Dear Parent:

Congratulations! Your child is taking the first steps on an exciting journey. The destination? Independent reading!

STEP INTO READING® will help your child get there. The program offers books at five levels that accompany children from their first attempts at reading to reading success. Each step includes fun stories, fiction and nonfiction, and colorful art. There are also Step into Reading Sticker Books, Step into Reading Math Readers, and Step into Reading Phonics Readers—a complete literacy program with something to interest every child.

Learning to Read, Step by Step!

Ready to Read Preschool–Kindergarten
• big type and easy words • rhyme and rhythm • picture clues
For children who know the alphabet and are eager to begin reading.

Reading with Help Preschool–Grade 1
• basic vocabulary • short sentences • simple stories
For children who recognize familiar words and sound out new words with help.

Reading on Your Own Grades 1–3
• engaging characters • easy-to-follow plots • popular topics
For children who are ready to read on their own.

Reading Paragraphs Grades 2–3
• challenging vocabulary • short paragraphs • exciting stories
For newly independent readers who read simple sentences with confidence.

Ready for Chapters Grades 2–4
• chapters • longer paragraphs • full-color art
For children who want to take the plunge into chapter books but still like colorful pictures.

STEP INTO READING® is designed to give every child a successful reading experience. The grade levels are only guides. Children will progress through the steps at their own speed, developing confidence in their reading. The F&P Text Level on the back cover serves as another tool to help you choose the right book for your child.

Remember, a lifetime love of reading starts with a single step!

To my two little polar babies, Hollie and Jill
—S.R.

To Tyler, Peter, David, and Hunter
—L.M.

Text copyright © 2000 by Susan Ring
Cover art and interior illustrations copyright © 2000 by Lisa McCue

All rights reserved. Published in the United States by Random House Children's Books,
a division of Penguin Random House LLC, New York. Originally published as *Polar Babies*
by Random House Children's Books, New York, in 2000.

Step into Reading, Random House, and the Random House colophon are registered
trademarks of Penguin Random House LLC.

Visit us on the Web!
StepIntoReading.com
randomhousekids.com

Educators and librarians, for a variety of teaching tools, visit us at RHTeachersLibrarians.com

Library of Congress Cataloging-in-Publication Data is available upon request.
ISBN 978-0-399-54954-0 (trade) — ISBN 978-0-399-54955-7 (lib. bdg.) — ISBN 978-0-399-55469-8 (ebook)

Printed in the United States of America

10 9 8 7 6 5 4 3 2

This book has been officially leveled by using the F&P Text Level Gradient™ Leveling System.

Random House Children's Books supports the First Amendment and celebrates the right to read.

POLAR BEAR BABIES

by Susan Ring

illustrated by Lisa McCue

Random House 🏠 New York

Wake up,
polar babies!
It is a big day.

Polar babies
learn to fish.

This polar baby
loves to fish.

This polar baby
loves to sleep!

Polar babies
learn to swim.

This polar baby

loves to swim.

This polar baby
loves to sleep!

Polar babies learn
to walk on the ice.

This polar baby
loves the ice.

This polar baby
loves to sleep!

Oh, no!

A big,
big polar bear!

Polar babies learn
to run!

Run, polar babies!
Run!

Polar babies run

over the ice…

...past the fishing hole...

...into the water...

...and back to
their safe, safe den!

Now <u>this</u> polar baby
wants to sleep.

What does this
polar baby want?

Another big day!